Volume 90 of the Yale Series of Younger Poets

Living in the Resurrection

T. Crunk

Foreword by James Dickey

Yale University Press   New Haven and London

Publication of this volume was made possible by a grant from the Guinzburg Fund.

Designed by Rebecca Gibb.
Set in Bembo type by Tseng Information Systems, Inc., Durham, North Carolina.
Printed in the United States of America by Thomson-Shore, Inc., Dexter, Michigan.

Library of Congress Cataloging-in-Publication Data
Crunk, Tony.
  Living in the Resurrection / T. Crunk ; foreword by James Dickey.
  p.   cm. — (Yale series of younger poets ; v. 90)
  ISBN 0-300-06525-6 (cloth : alk. paper). — ISBN 0-300-06526-4 (pbk. : alk. paper)
  I. Title.   II. Series.
  PS3553.R7855L5   1995
  813'.54—dc20   95-12681
                                                                      CIP
A catalogue record for this book is available from the British Library.

The paper in this book meets the guidelines for permanence and durability of the Committee on Production Guidelines for Book Longevity of the Council on Library Resources.

10   9   8   7   6   5   4   3   2   1

for Deborah
with whom all things are possible
thanks to GO/CW/SKW/WGS/JD

Contents

Foreword

"Home is burning in me," his epigraph from Lucille Clifton, acts as Tony Crunk's compass; over the years it wavers, but

> like the needle verging to the north
> [it] trembles and trembles into certainty.
> (W. S. Landor)

The poet's central concern is the search—quest—for Home, one that takes him from childhood in a small town in Western Kentucky to a sparsely populated—almost wilderness—environment in Montana.

During these voyagings, almost random ones at times, a religious orientation begins and shapes itself into poems. In his work there is a touching and accurate reliance on primitive spontaneity; Mr. Crunk always goes with his instincts, often sparked and fed by a Baptist upbringing—

> my shadow
> the cross
> that one day will bear me away

—and with his equally instinctive reliance on the ritual magics of the tribe, creates poetry with a highly personal, rough-hewn, metaphysics-from-simple-materials feel.

> I have made myself a coffin with a glass lid.
> By the door of my grave house
>
> I have set a cement angel and a stone jug.
> When I see the host coming down, the lid will fly open
>
> and I will sail out into the air like a locust.
> If I am called above, the angel will help me on my way.
>
> If I have to go below, I will grab my jug
> and fill it with water somewhere on the road down.

One thinks with increasing conviction that here is that rare phenomenon, a writer of instinctive formal vision. His real reverence for the simple objects of the everyday world, their ability to present cup, tree, and hand both as they seem and as they are with a kind of mystical iconic starkness, is a quality uniquely Mr. Crunk's. That

this starkness eventually begins to warp into the surreal and ulti-
mately windows into the Luminous Beyond is additional sanction
for gratitude.

The quest, here, is reminiscent of the Crow Indian figure of
the earth-diver: the explorer of dark and hidden things shot through
with the life force; he is the seed-brother, the mixer, the one who
makes things fecund. The human being does not address or learn
how to live with, to love and to use, by getting away from the im-
mediate reality of the things of this world but by diving into them.
This happens in many places for Mr. Crunk, but he always brings
something back, no matter what the buried light divulges to him,
whether fearful, exultant, or sad.

Always, beginning from his rural Kentucky homeland through
all of his wanderings and earth-divings, his return from darkness
to light with a secret revelation, the poet's orientation is land- and
home- and family-based, and his primary art is also that of his homeland's religion—of Southern gospel music and homiletics—com-
bined with visions of spontaneity and intuition.

In the gospel tradition, the heavenly home that awaits at
the end of this life is most often cast in the imagery of the homestead we have left behind in our wanderings. In this tradition our
simplest "real-world" experience is nostalgia for our place of ori-
gin—our original family and childhood—transformed into the most
profound spiritual longing we can have. Crossed with the legendary,
the mythic, the tribal, the gospel tradition takes on qualities of the
universe revealed. One may be sure that, through all the false starts,
the dippings and waverings of the compass needle, the true Place will
finally be given. As with Cavafy's (and Homer's) wanderer,

> *if you find her poor, Ithaca has not defrauded you.*
> *With the great wisdom you have gained, with so much experience,*
> *You must surely have understood by now what Ithacas mean.*
>
> ("Ithaca")

Come to the final homestead, which on first encounter very
well might have hit the poet with an explosion of rightness and
finality after his years on the road—Cain's Mill, Barkley Lake—

the quester is certain that for a glittering moment the thing has happened; in a flash of revelation all the way-points of the journey appear.

> *Meantime, every day I pray — O Lord*
> *teach me that I am but earth,*
>
> *a hollow vessel of clay,*
> *only a wisp of thy breath against my emptiness.*

3

> *They have yet to figure out*
> *the name of the church*
>
> *two men diving in Barkley Lake*
> *around Cain's Mill a few years ago*
>
> *found the whole steeple of*
> *cross and all*
>
> *half-buried in the mud shallows.*

These revelations stand there in the first and last light, to be repeated later, when familiarity comes. Farm-singing Southern Christianity and the ever-present shaman give the bodying-forth of what life is composed of before it becomes our daily bewilderment: the true festive harvest-home of existence, rooted in peace and flowering in elation.

James Dickey

Acknowledgments

Acknowledgment is made to the following journals for poems that originally appeared in them:

CutBank "Blues for Home"

Gulfstream Magazine "The Tent," "After Visiting Home for Christmas"

Hampden-Sydney Poetry Review "Post-Metaphysical Man at Home," "Winter"

High Plains Literary Review "Earthly Garments"

Laurel Review "Christmas Morning"

New Virginia Review "The Mirror"

Paris Review "Redemption"

Pikeville Review "Summer Evening"

Plains Poetry Journal "Baptism," "Reliquaria"

Poet Lore "Souvenirs"

Poetry Northwest "For Sallie Youngs"

Quarterly West "Sunday Afternoon, Waiting for the Funeral to Start"

Talking River Review "August," "Story," "Prison Train"

Timbuktu "Visiting a Lost Aunt at the Jefferson Davis Hotel, Elkton"

Virginia Quarterly Review "Leaving"

Living in the Resurrection

home is burning in me *Lucille Clifton*

Earthly Garments

Christmas Morning

The cold reveals everything
between thick sky and the raw furrows
of last year's gardens up and down the alley—
houses drawn and closed,
two dogs chained to a fencepost sleeping
on bare dirt, brown smoke and ash
rising from the rusted oil barrel
where my brother and I are burning the wrapping paper
behind my grandmother's shed.

Every year we do this, every year
scuffing at the gravel and coal chips
to keep warm, until we are called for dinner.
And every year I look closer
into his clear, unhindered face
and think that we are finally growing older—
one of us
still saved by the blood of the lamb,
one still waiting for the dumb to speak.

Souvenirs

for my father

Through the mirror
I can see you reading
your new testament before bed,
putting it away in the dresser drawer
where you keep

the tin box of foreign coins
and the hand-tinted postcards
of Italy
you brought home from the Navy
in 1954.

We lie awake
my brother and I
listening to you on the back steps
singing
only half to yourself
a snatch of an old miner's song
that goes:

up every day
in the dawn's early light

to go down in a hole
where it's already night

it's already night
boys it's already night,

and through the window
I watch the fireflies
among the trees,
which,
you told us once,
were dead people lighting cigarettes.

February

The copperhead and moccasin
are sleeping
vein deep in the blood of winter.

Magnolias
rub their swollen hands together
attempting to discover fire.

Blue shirts
my traveling clothes
once so carefully mended

now shredding
on scarecrows we forgot to bring in
in November.

I walk among them
now, in the dusting snow and moonlight
my arms stretched out—

my shadow
the cross
that one day will bear me away.

3 drms.

picking through the manna
one morning
looking for the small
white stone
engraved with my name

praying at my window
come down
angel come down
into the circle of light

waiting in a station
among the scatterlings
and strandlings
for the train that brings lost fathers
home to their children

Reliquaria

1 *Found Hand-Painted on a Tin Flue Cover*

Ribbon of black crape
draped on a door knob

like broken strings
hanging from a loom

with the words: *Weep not.*
What do I need of this world?

2 *S. P. Dinsmoor Describes His Tomb*

I have made myself a coffin with a glass lid.
By the door of my grave house

I have set a cement angel and a stone jug.
When I see the host coming down, the lid will fly open

and I will sail out into the air like a locust.
If I am called above, the angel will help me on my way.

If I have to go below, I will grab my jub
and fill it with water somewhere on the road down.

Meantime, every day I pray—O Lord
teach me that I am but earth,

a hollow vessel of clay,
only a wisp of thy breath against my emptiness.

3

They have yet to figure out
the name of the church

two men diving in Barkley Lake
around Cain's Mill a few years ago

found the whole steeple of
cross and all

half-buried in the mud shallows.

Charity

Buying shirts
at the second
baptist thrift shop:
quiet hostel

for old coats
resting
too tired to hold
their bodies

anymore
on their repetitious journeys
from the dead
back to the dying.

August

Twilight sifts down
into the peach trees in the yard

and the roses stir
at the hint of rain in a dry month.

My mother and father
are repotting plants on the back steps—

the dumb cane and peace lily
job's tears and pennyroyal.

A handful of bats
folds and unfolds around a hemlock

on the hill
where the wind is whispering itself to sleep.

Nothing is redeemed
except by accident.

Sunday Afternoon, Waiting for the Funeral to Start

Sun on the highway
percolating tar to the asphalt's surface —
sweat of the earth.

Heat ghosts shimmering
as they rise. Yellow jackets
stitching time among the chicory.

Moss swaying in the shallows
where the churchyard
frays out into the creek.

Blue dragonfly lifting
setting down lifting
unable to carry its shadow with it.

Earthly Garments

Late afternoon
on Grave Tree Hill
waiting for the sun to go off—

grasshoppers take flight across the hayfield
whole generations
migrating back and forth

flecks of chaff and seed
drift up with the heat
drift down.

From here I can still make out the peafowls
stepping across the driveway—
little death witches

—and the slow fire of rust
scorching the tin roofs of the houses and the barns
the cribs and the empty oil tanks and the silos,

returning to air
all that would endure
all that I would leave behind.

The darkness tightens.
A cricket counting
zero to one million.

A breeze lifts slightly
the bit of rag
caught on a talon of barbed wire.

2

The fire I have built at wood's edge
must look
to the plane passing overhead,
too high for me to hear it, like a candle

lit for the lost
or sainted. And I remember
that when the ashes would drift over
from Paradise plant

my brother
would say they were the ashes of dead people,
that your body turned to coal when you were buried,
which they burned

to make electricity, and I would wonder
if the souls drifted over with them,
if they could look down and see us
writing our names

in the ashes that settled on the car windows,
and I would wonder if at night
the lights of houses, of lanterns
hanging in the barns

looked like constellations
falling away below, or if they looked
like the lamps, still burning,
of towns that have disappeared

to the bottom of a TVA lake,
which I'd heard them say you can see
off beneath your boat
as you glide over the black water.

3

By ember-light and ash-light
I am reading my future

in the palm of the sweet gum leaf.
I am seeking the vein

that is the road I would follow
called The Way of Endless Partings.

I am ticking off the stations
that are nothing to me:

Missing Persons, Forgotten Land
Accidents of Illumination

Bitter Crossings.
I am leaving I

am leaving
under the wing of night.

And why should I return
if only to remember

I am nothing
if only to be washed

and made whole again
& again?

Discursions

Visiting a Lost Aunt at the Jefferson Davis Hotel, Elkton

All my father said when he hung up the phone was, "Well I guess Wanda has found her way back." We wait for him now in the small lobby while he looks for somebody to help us. There's a coat tree, a newspaper rack, a cigarette machine. There's a big chair in the corner where they shine shoes, but nobody's shining shoes on Sunday. I have never been inside a hotel before.

He comes back, leads us up the carpeted stairs and into a hallway— a window open at the end of it, a thin veil of rainwater rolling down off the eaves. We find number 28 and knock.

I have never seen Aunt Wanda before. She opens the door, wearing shorts on Sunday morning, and we go in. She hugs my mother, then my father—she's sorry we had to come all that way in the rain—sets a suitcase in the closet to get it out of the way—she would've called last night but was out late with some people she had looked up.

There are only two chairs, so my mother sits on the bed with my brother and me. Aunt Wanda is sorry it's so hot in there, but they didn't even have a window fan they could give her. She would offer us something to drink, but there isn't any ice. They all light cigarettes, sharing the one ashtray. Rainwater is rolling off the eaves outside her window, too.

Aunt Wanda talks a while about my brother and me, reaches over and pats my ankle, my mother smoothes my hair back off my forehead. My father tells about his new job, driving mail to Bowling Green. Aunt Wanda tells about somebody in Louisville—I guess he would have been my uncle. She asks my father about their cousin Dewey. She asks about the home place, but doesn't think she'll have time to go out.

Finally, my father tells her how their father, my grandfather, died. At the VA Hospital in Nashville, in a room overlooking the parking lot. Calling out for three days that his legs were on fire. Calling out for water.

Aunt Wanda shakes the ashtray, watching the ashes and butts sift back and forth. I'm watching, too, wishing I were home. I would spend the afternoon picking the shells of katydids off of trees. Dropping them one by one into the gutter stream that would be running by the sidewalk. Walking along beside them as they floated down the street—my ghost fleet, vanishing through the grating of the storm drain on the corner.

Prison Train

At night, the signs on the buildings move with light: horses running in front of a wagon, a man with a satchel waving his arm, a big Coke sparkling out into a glass. On the way to the depot my brother reads them to me: Coach-and-Four Motel, Winfree's Home Accident and Life, Enjoy refreshing Coca-Cola.

We have come to town to see the prison train. It picks up convicts in different cities in this end of the state and carries them to the Pen in Eddyville. This is the last one—my father guesses they'll just use police cars after this—and people are going down to see it.

When we pull into the lot, people are leaning and sitting on their cars—a couple of them have their radios on. My mother doesn't want to be there, says it's pitiful enough for those boys to be going where they're going without all this. So she waits in the car. Walking up to where the crowd is gathering, I look back and see her face and see the thin line of blue smoke rising from a cigarette she has tossed out onto the gravel.

After we find a place on the platform, everything is over fast: The ground rumbling, getting louder. The horn blatting and the headlight swinging around from behind the lumberyard. The giant engine pulling the curve, wheels squalling, my father's grip tightening on my shoulders. The passenger car stopping right in front of us, my brother reading the old-timey lettering to me— Kentucky State Penitentiary System. People talking loud over the noise. Whole families standing on the platform counting the faces in the lighted windows . . .

Visiting the Site of One of the
First Churches My Grandfather Pastored

My mother said later that, to the shovel operators, we must have
looked like some delegation from out of town that couldn't find the
picnic. Or else the funeral. Not so bad my brother and me jumping
the fence, and my father, but then my mother, and all of us helping
my grandfather over, and finally my grandmother deciding she
wanted to see, too.

Then all of us standing together at the rim of the pit in our Sunday
clothes, sun reflecting off my grandmother's black patent purse, a
few trees still hanging on nearby, roots exposed, like tentacles, like
the earth is shrinking under them. The smell of sulphur.

The giant bucket scoops up through the rocks and dirt, the shovel
swings around, the bucket empties, and the whole thing swings
back, the noise taking an extra second to reach us. I am watching the
two men inside, expecting them to notice us, to wave us away
because we don't belong there, but they don't. They must be used
to it.

Years later I will remember my grandfather saying that they strip
away the land but all they put back is the dirt. Maybe plant a few
scrub pine. "Good for nothing any more," he says now, turning to
go back to the car. "Good for nothing except holding the rest of
the world together."

It looks almost blue in the sun, the piece of coal I have picked up
to take home for a souvenir.

Summer Evening

for my mother

The streetlight at the corner flickers on. Begins to hum. Starlings
settle into the maples up and down the street. Above the fan
whirring in a window next door, the sound of plates being set on
a table. You are sitting on the concrete block steps, hugging your
white knees. I am kneeling at the corner of the house, trying to
replace the bricks that have come loose and fallen out from the
foundation—the air from underneath the porch breathes out cool
and damp. I can barely hear the radio from back in the kitchen. I can
barely hear you humming along. When I look up I can see the blind
girl at her window in the house across the street.

2

In one of the only photographs I have of you, you are maybe nine
or ten. It must be around 1940 or '41. You are standing at the side of
a house, bright sun splayed out across the clapboard, a kerosene lamp
on a table in the window. You are squinting behind your glasses. You
are wearing thick socks, even though it's summer, I guess to keep
your second- or third-hand shoes from rubbing. You are holding a
bottle up to the camera—the label says "Waterman's Ink." It's half
full of coins. A small suitcase is standing in the dirt and cinders
beside you.

3

A dry breeze rustles the top leaves of the trees, heat making way for
a late shower. In a few minutes we will hear the first thunder and go
inside.

In a few years we will no longer live there. In a few more it will be
a house I drive by to look at when I visit home. In a few more I will
stop driving by, and in a few more I will have nowhere to visit.

And there is no belonging in a borrowed world. No belonging until,
at last, our eyes adjust and we see, finally, all that we have lost, and all
that's been returned to us: that evening—were you thinking of me
then, to wish me safety on my journey, as tonight I think of you and
wish you peace on yours?

Visiting My Grandmother at Oak Lawn

In a niche above the main doors is a statue of a saint, his left arm broken off at the elbow, that they've never bothered to replace or take down. Before it was a nursing home it was the old TB hospital, and there isn't an oak tree anymore within three blocks.

Today my grandmother's roommate isn't in, so she is alone. She is sitting in her chair by the window, and she recognizes me as soon as I go in. We talk while I open the curtains for her, straighten the things on her nightstand. I go for a pitcher of fresh ice water.

When I return she is worried again that I haven't been saved, wants me to tell her again about being baptized. So I do, even though I have to tell the same story every other time I come —

I tell her she was standing in the shade of a honey locust on the bank, beside my mother and father and brother, when my grand-father led us across the strip of pasture to the river. There were five of us, I think, and we had taken turns changing clothes in Verna Woosley's tool shed. I tell her she was wearing a purple, white-dotted dress. She says she remembers, and remembers singing "Shall We Gather at the River" as we moved down into the water, as my grandfather waded out waist-deep, into the sunlight.

I tell her that when it was my turn, and I was standing next to him, I could see minnows darting at our legs, could see our shadows on the water behind us. I could feel his strong arm against my back. Then he put his handkerchief over my mouth and said in my ear, "Don't breathe now," and lay me back into the water. It felt, I tell her, like my shadow had swallowed me.

She has turned to face the window again by now. She is nodding slowly. "Baptized into union with Christ Jesus," she says, the way she does sometimes when she's been listening. "Baptized into his death," she says, quoting Romans.

We talk a while longer, mostly about the rest of the family. I give her the shampoo and nut bread my mother has sent, look to see if there is anything else she needs. Then I call for one of the aides to come and keep her in her room, otherwise she will follow me out to the car, begging me to take her home.

I hear her calling after me as I walk the long corridor toward the small glass door at the end, which looks as though it's getting larger as I get closer. Or else it's me, getting smaller. And I've never told her what my brother told me after he had done it—that when you come up out of the river, your soul is new, and you know why hell is fire and why heaven is blue, like water.

After Visiting Home for Christmas

A few rows in front of me on the bus, two boys, maybe ten or eleven, are waving at cars that pass us on the Interstate, trying to get people to wave back, falling into their seat to laugh about it. They're with the group of deaf kids that gets on in Louisville on Sundays, on their way back to the State School in Danville. The sky is thickening with twilight and low clouds, a few flakes.

Just beyond Midway a car passes, the boys wave, and the car slows down, staying even with the bus. The woman on the passenger side is gesturing to the boys, they're gesturing back—it takes me a second to realize they are talking to each other. Three or four of the other kids come around to watch.

They talk that way for several miles. Then the woman waves good-bye, and the boys wave, it getting too dark by then for them to see . . .

Lost Music

Tomorrow we will leave
For a land of strangers. *Edier Segura*

Blues for Home

All that remains
is this wooden chair
sitting in the shade of an elm

blood of the earth
lisping from root to root
below me

a few bricks
scattered among the thistle.

All that remains
is to rub my hands across them
patiently—

the erasure of my fingerprints
is all that remains now
for my perfection.

Three Hymns

1 *Pilgrim Song*

Willows stringing their harps along the river
stars like nail holes in a tin roof

flametips of the sumac lighting the way.
Only my shadow passing over the red dust

and still the host of the air, host of the ransomed light
in their beautiful wallpaper robes

calling, *Come little stranger. A little farther.*
Make peace here with what we have found for you.

2 Orphan Song

Look, mother. New souls are flashing in the river.
—Only a handful of minnows, the color of copper.

Look, mother. Petals of darkness, clenched at our waists.
—Only our shadows floating on the surface.

Look, father. The hand in the water, still beckoning.
—Only a leaf from the sweet gum. Now another.

Listen. The sound of graves bursting.
—One by one, we are crossing into Beulah-land.

3 Prisoner Song

> At nightfall the resurrected meet on mountain paths. *Georg Trakl*

Below: the riverline of honey locusts,
garments I've discarded somewhere on the bank.

Field of dry thistle dry bittersweet,
a breeze walking. A house.

The orphan bent under lamplight
sifting a family Bible, the marriages

and generations, seeking his first name.
Two men clearing fencerows near a barn,

burning brush, wings of gray ash ascending.
Above: fist of the moon unclenching.

Refrain: rockaway comfort rockaway.

The Mirror

1 *Hieroglyphs*

The sheaf of wheat
is dancing

the wheel is labor
the hand sleep

the tree is this
one black tree at twilight

black cows
grazing near the pond

circles breaking
to the surface of the water

2 *The Tent*

Each night I crawl in to sleep
and dream I had been born in a boat
and had grown up wondering how land feels
how deep it is
how far into it I could sink

3 *Negation: Its Origin and Uses*

The moon is
the hole in the sky
it seeps through

covering the pasture
with blue emptiness
dissolving the house with

sleep like a lozenge
in night's throat.
Waking, the web of

space returning,
we see what we think
we always see—the sun's

green light, dew,
yellow spider on
the blackberry cane.

4 The Mirror

Then I needed only
a house to put it in

took the pieces where I found them

window plucked from clouds
door drawn up
from the bottom of a stream
mantelpiece carved from tree and rock

this is a world
I said
and the man looking into it

and the man looking out of it
bag of breath
geometry of twigs
blue shirt

Two Reflections

1 Story

after Ursachi

At dawn the snails set out on their journeys
each carrying its bead of time.

In the asylum the lamps are being extinguished.
The last surviving Euclidean

sits on his bed, waiting to be bathed.
On the table a poem begins,

"Darkness and light: a spiral, a constellation . . ."
The snails move forward.

The sea advances at continent's edge.
There's a chance of snow.

2 *Post-Metaphysical Man at Home*

We are what remains,
sparks and shards of a lost music,

mathematical points whose only qualities
are their relations to each other.

He looks up from having written this
and sees, outside, a bat

like a thin black hand
sailing above the trees

above the tears of yellow light
hung in the windows of the houses.

Redemption

But thy dead live, their bodies will rise again. They that sleep in the earth will awake and shout for joy; and the earth will bring those long dead to birth again. *Isaiah 26:19*

Objects of Belief

Lying awake, watching the moon heal over,
counting all that is mine, but not my own—
breath, and the shapes my pale hands
turn in the air, and the things of my father
I still carry with me: a tin box
of foreign coins, a leather hunting coat . . .

White mist rising from the pond,
cows bawling in the distance
like angels moving slowly across the fields,
fireflies tapping out around them
the five laws of darkness:
desire . . . atomistic . . . return . . .

For Sallie Youngs

Wallpaper frays, curls down in the ceiling's corners
where the room has drawn smaller into itself
like the old woman sleeping, the caned chair at the window,
the clock's wooden notches in the silence
vigilant, exhausted.

                    If you should wake
at dawn, as the house takes up its memory,
as lost shadows begin to wander
in the blue-sooted mirror above the coal grate,
lie still: already the smooth hand of light
reaches in, already the procession of clouds flies over.

Leaving

Were there such an end as destination
I could say that I was leaving,
could imagine friends gathered on the street below,
cheering maybe, waving maps tied to sticks.
But there isn't. There is only expansion and contraction
like infinity, or a dime on the sidewalk,
like a letter I found in a corner of the empty room
I am moving out of, a letter I didn't mail
that begins, "Dear S. — Guilt is the wound that never stops healing:
at times I want to look outside and see my daughter
standing beneath the ash tree and the stars,
a sparkler hissing blue and yellow in her two hands.
But the window is missing, lost,
lying in a field where someone passing
could look down into it and see the faces
rising up through the earth
and sinking back. . . ." A tiny, well-formed cloud
hovers in the space between my eye and the page.
I imagine I have inhaled the sky,
that I grow larger. I imagine that one day
I may grow large enough to fill my body.

Baptism

The river is a wound in the earth.
The river is the clay-red blood of love
pulling its silence through us.

Hymnal of sunlight, black script of trees—
a hand passes over bereft of its shadow.

And the soul is a small glass boat setting out.

(A vine hangs down into the water:
a strand of lightning ossified.)

Redemption

1

Driving through the mining counties
Green River to Central City
light of dawn like water
shadows rising to the surface

going back for my grandmother's funeral:
in Muhlenberg
a raised welt of railroad tracks
bitter porches emptying to morning

and beneath the skewed abandoned
cross of a telephone pole
a woman with a tin scuttle

gathering coal that had fallen from the trains
dried clots of earth's blood.

2

Afternoon at my father's house
sun filling empty flower pots by the coal shed

watching the hollyhocks the roses and mimosa
recalling one of my grandfather's sermons:

how the souls will one day set out
to find their new bodies

how they will leave behind this hollow earth
swirling with ice and rags

I imagine them rising above the blistering corn
above the dust of the dry rows the chaff settling

and all they can see from the air
is the smallest thing: a piece of straw

caught in the planks of the barn door
a black wasp clinging to the kitchen screen.

3

Awake that night in the spare room
which once was mine

streetlamp through the curtains
lit sparkler of moths
radio from an upstairs window

fear of nakedness of insignificance
the corridors of my narrow life

the viewing room was carpeted and modern

counting sadly backward to myself.

4

Moon in the spines of the hawthorn
clouds amethyst and omniscient
hands of the clock again moving
toward morning and I picture headlights
tracing through the cemetery as through a maze:

when our souls lie waiting in their beds
our bodies
awaiting the end of baptism by earth

and we picture somewhere above us
the house we were born in
can see the hydrangeas and impatiens by the steps
a crown of gnats hovering above the four o'clocks
a red bee bowing into one of the yellow blossoms
and through an open window a lamp
curtains reaching up into the room

what peace will lift us
whispering what hope
who want only to rise to the surface
as through water

what peace when we want to return
not set out
when we want only to step up onto that windy porch
to step back through that fiery door?

Winter

Night settles through the house.
The last coil of smoke
lifts like a moan through the chimney.

On the kitchen table
the light inside the egg comes on,
the faint tapping resumes.

Benediction

Benediction for the Invalid Hour

Until the baptism of fishes,
                until
fire in the rock,
          until deserts
and rust—
        somewhere amid
all the gatherings
           and recedings, somewhere
between a slow death
           and slow life,
somewhere above
          the implacable landscape,
a glimpse of something
            white in the air . . .

Constellations

the caravan of exiles
has camped in the valley
of cenobitic blue spruce

among the tents and wagons
a few gods
tending the fires
reading the ashes

    *

angel wings
flashing

is what my grandmother

called heat lightning

    *

tongue of flame—

the lucent
yellow parabola
on
the wall above my lamp

    *

the last load of empty hoppers
on its way back

walks Mannington trestle
at midnight

shaving sparks of rust
off the rails

then flattens it out across the Barrens
and up into the south Peabody fields

like
ladders striding out of a whirlwind

    *

the nails
of the cross of Jesus

    burning
are ~~rusting~~

*

the moon is
a chip from a bone handled knife

the moon is called
Orphan's Torch

the moon in its phases
is a musical notation

a shape note hymn
that goes:

listen
I will come for you

by rushlight

Reunion

What we mistook for flight
was only the long struggle
to surface, and we arrive
at a place familiar as a socket—
sitting by a dirt road, watching wind
bristle the raw corn stubble,

discussing gravity and how,
with the invention of dust,
things began to pick up speed,
how October lays bare
the age of the world, how we
may yet find the word we seek,

which may be a labyrinth
with nothing at its center,
or a snowy egret that will rise
above the houses and the wires,
or which may again be the root
that, pulled up, lies twisting in our hands . . .

Notes

Reliquaria: S. P. Dinsmoor Describes His Tomb
S. P. Dinsmoor was architect and builder of a monumental concrete
sculpture garden in Lucas, Kansas, under construction 1907–32. Most
of the lines of this poem are taken from statements of Dinsmoor's
found in Gregg Blasdel and Philip Larson, "S. P. Dinsmoor's Garden
of Eden," in *Naives and Visionaries* (New York: Dutton, 1974).

Two Reflections: Post-Metaphysical Man at Home
Lines 3 and 4 are adapted from a passage on page 8 of Alan R. White's
Philosophy of Mind (Random House, 1967).

Epigraphs

Living in the Resurrection
From Lucille Clifton, "moses," © 1987 by Lucille Clifton. Rpt. from
Good Woman: Poems and a Memoir, 1969–1980, by Lucille Clifton, with
permission of BOA Editions.

Lost Music
Edier Segura was "a well-known dance musician and singer in the
Segura Brothers Band," recorded by John and Alan Lomax in 1934 in
Delcambre, Louisiana, as part of the Library of Congress's Archive
of Folk Music project. The quoted line is from "Le Pays des étrangers,"
trans. Barry Jean Ancelet, as it appears on *Louisiana Cajun and Creole
Music, 1934: The Lomax Recordings,* © 1987 by Swallow Records, Ville
Platte, Louisiana.

Three Hymns: Prisoner Song
From Georg Trakl, "Helian," trans. Christopher Middleton. Rpt.
from *Modern German Poetry,* ed. and trans. Michael Hamburger and
Christopher Middleton (New York: Grove, 1962), with permission
of Christopher Middleton.